Keeping Faith in the 21st Century

*Encouraging Respectful Discussions of 4th Century
Beliefs with 21st Century Minds and Hearts*

by Joe Norquist, M.D.

DORRANCE
PUBLISHING CO
EST. 1920
PITTSBURGH, PENNSYLVANIA 15238

Dorrance Publishing Co
585 Alpha Drive
Pittsburgh, PA 15238
Visit our website at *www.dorrancebookstore.com*

ISBN: 978-1-6461-0086-6
eISBN: 978-1-6461-0911-1

Table of Contents

Dedication

I dedicate this book to the memory of my dear wife, Marilyn, who encouraged me even when she sometimes disagreed with me.

I am very thankful for the 66 mostly happy years of our very interesting and adventurous life together. She was hit with Alzheimer's disease and passed away on August 1st, 2019. She wasn't able to read my completed book but I received much encouragement from her. I praise God for her life.

Acknowledgment

I want to thank Elise d'Entremont, Technical Instructor, Editor, Writer and Consultant, for advice and suggestions given to me, a new author. By sometimes shortening sentences or avoiding the overly repetitive use of certain words, the book became more readable. She convinced me to base my book mainly on my own life-experiences as high school and college student, medical student, famiily doctor, medical missionary in Tanzania, and as a husband, father and grandfather, rather than quoting deep theological studies of the scholars. "Save the serious theology for your second book," she would say to me.

Introduction

Keeping Faith in the 21st Century was written with the hope of stimulating conversation among Christians about faith and doubt. I continue my own life journey with my own questions accrued during my long life as a student, as a medical doctor, as a missionary doctor, as a filmmaker, as a father, as a husband, and as a Christian.

It is my sincere belief that Progressive Revelation did not stop with the New Testament or the writing of our creeds. Progressive Revelation has traditionally been defined by Christians as a fuller revelation of God in the Biblical scriptures written later (New Testament) than earlier sections (Hebrew Scripture). This definition not only denigrates Hebrew integrity but also ignores vast amounts of knowledge, inspiration, and revelation through the many centuries since that time.

I'm convinced Christians with doubts can still be followers of Jesus. Many friends who are pastors tell me my ideas may not be heretical, yet avoid preaching topics that contradict teachings of the greater church for the sake of their members. My best friend who became my brother-in-law, Pastor Dick Borgstrom, told me he had learned from a seminary professor that one should never take away a belief without replacing it with another sustainable concept. This could be a challenge.

Our twenty-first century minds function differently from those of the first and fourth centuries when the Christian Bible's New Testament and creeds, respectively, were established. Thankfully, we have the advantage of science, history, more recent theology, and our own life experiences to aid in our understanding of faith and the Bible. The writers of the Bible and creeds did not know about gravity or lack of oxygen in the upper atmosphere. It was easy to accept someone's walking on water or floating up to heaven. In biblical times, the people were positive the earth was the center of the universe. When Galileo and his improved telescope in 1610 verified Copernicus' theory of the earth revolving around the sun rather than the world being the center of creation, he was ordered by the Inquisition to renounce his writings. Pope Urban III placed him under arrest and surveillance until Galileo's death. A Christian burial in his family tomb in the *Santa Croce* Church in Florence, Italy was forbidden until fifty-five years after his death, when permission was granted. So his body is resting in that church today. In my travels, I was able to visit Galileo's tomb in Florence. In 1992, the Roman Catholic Church finally exonerated Galileo for his "heretical" writings, 359 years after his death!

Early generations did not know about conception, sperm, ova, chromosomes, what caused lightning, thunder, hurricanes, rainbows, or most diseases. They didn't understand the winds and seasons, planets and stars, or the existence of other people living in other continents.

In *Keeping Faith in the 21st Century*, I discuss many of these issues and how I have solved each question or puzzle to my own satisfaction. You will see how my life began imbedded with deep, simple, fundamentalist emphasis. As I experienced more of life, my understanding of calling or vocation changed. During my high school days, I felt increasingly God calling me to be a missionary. It was almost as if I had heard God's voice. As I experienced more of life, my understanding of calling or vocation changed. It may well be for everyone, religious or secular, a call or vocation may be a meaningful dedication to the career most suitable for each person, processing in this way:

- Workers are needed in a certain worthy field of employment.
- An individual has a keen interest in that vocation.
- The person has the abilities to learn to do that kind of work.

It seems to me this combination will fit any call to almost any vocation. A calling may not be a direct vocal guidance from God. But with contemplation and prayer, there will be more assurance of making the right choices.

The changes occurred in my life one-by-one through the years. Each change usually made me more liberal but actually also more comfortable, honest, and reconciled by believing the Bible, science, and some modern theology.

Some time, at your convenience, I would appreciate your turning to my life story, "About the Author," found at the back pages of this book, so you may have a better understanding of how I have come to my conclusions. Now, if you have already read my life history or have chosen to read it later, we now continue with Chapter One.

Chapter One -
Beginning with Genesis

According to my saintly Sunday School teacher from sixth to ninth grades, God created human beings on the Sixth Day as perfect, without disease or sin, and humans would never die. Adam was made from clay, Eve from one of Adam's ribs. Then came "The Fall" and everything changed. Now there was sin. Now there was death. Later, after people had multiplied and were wicked, God sent a huge flood to destroy all people except several devout humans, Noah, Noah's wife, and their three sons and their wives. When the waters lowered, God made a rainbow across the sky as a covenant there would never again be such a flood.

In my second year of high school, I learned in Physics that a rainbow is made by the refraction and reflection of light through millions of tiny prismatic droplets in the cloudy sky. These droplets, individually and collectively, change white light from the sun into the colors of the rainbow: red, orange, yellow, green, blue, indigo, and violet. The writers of the Bible didn't know this, so they needed a story to fit the wonder of a beautiful rainbow! I still thrill and thank God for every rainbow I see.

During my thirteenth year of life, I read through the entire Bible on a regular, assigned schedule of weekdays and Sundays. The Navigators Bible memorization program was a fun way to memorize many Bible verses. The Navigators furnished small cards with a Bible verse to memorize on one side and the verse's Biblical location on the other side. The verses were all from the King James Bible, making it difficult for me now to memorize the same verses in newer translations.

The first conflict in my faith started in the fourth grade at Gladstone School on Frost Avenue in Gladstone, a county suburb of Saint Paul, Minnesota. Our science book displayed a picture of an ape and a short explanation how scientists were thinking humans and chimpanzees evolved slowly through millions of years from the same ancestor. I showed the book to my parents that evening. The next day I walked up to my teacher's desk and said politely, "Mrs. Hendrickson, we don't believe this."

She replied, wisely, "That's okay, Joey, you don't have to believe this. It's just what some scientists are saying how it may have happened."

That satisfied me for several years. I didn't need to listen to scientists talking about evolution.

My second year of college included the elective course Evolution 101 which taught the class that every relevant science, including anthropology, paleontology, embryology, comparative anatomy, biology, geology, archeology, and astronomy had concluded evolution was a fact, not just a theory. Humans were developing probably from the same ancestor as the chimpanzee, probably in Africa, to become *homo sapiens* 70,000 to 100,000 years ago. It was remarkable how the universe and human life were created. I did not see a conflict. God is still Creator of the Universe. Now we know more how humans came into existence.

Since there were people living and dying in almost all continents many years before Adam and Eve existed, there had obviously been death and evidence of primeval murder, and therefore sin, in humans throughout all time. *We are by nature sinful and unclean* (from Lutheran liturgical prayer). Sin and death are part of human nature. On several continents there is paleontological evidence of family structure and some marital arrangements. It may not be fair to insist God first instituted marriage in the Garden of Eden.

In 1971, Marilyn and I took our four children back to Tanzania. The older ones, Steve (seventeen) and Kathy (fifteen), remembered their childhood there and re-lived some of their experiences. Our third child, Judy, visited her birthplace at Kiomboi in Tanzania. Our youngest son, Doug, finally saw what he had only heard about or had seen in family photographs.

On the same safari, we drove to the Oldevai Gorge in the Great Rift Valley where we saw the excavations and displays where Louis and Mary Leakey, with their sons, discovered some very old near-human artifacts. We saw some primitive tools and a skull and upper teeth of a person they labeled later *Australopithecus boi-sei,* who had lived some 1.75 million years ago. What an education for our family to see such rare sites where early humans actually lived! The site also had some *Homo habilis* as well as *Homo sapiens* (modern humans) from about 17,000 years ago when these humans settled in the area. I was happy just being there. I wasn't uneasy about seeing artifacts in the development of the human species. By that time, at age forty-two, I had learned to reconcile differences between science, enlightenment, and faith. Science can be demonstrated and sometimes proven while not teaching us about love, mercy, patience, forgiveness, or joy. Every time I have been able to reconcile why there are differences between my faith beliefs and my newly-learned certainties, I have felt a freedom and peace.

Chapter Two -
The Nature of God

In cartoons, God is often depicted as an old man with a long, gray beard standing on a cloud and throwing a shaft of lightning at the earth. In conversations, God is sometimes casually referred to as "the man upstairs," "the gods," "fate," or "somebody up there". Since we do not and cannot know the exact nature of God, we search the Scriptures for some answers. The Bible says, "God is Spirit." (John 4:14). "The Spirit of God dwells within you." Romans 8:9. "God is Love." (I John 4:16). "God is my strength." (Isa 12:2). None of these descriptions tell us God has a voice, body, hands, feet, eyes, or a heart. Many churches now are trying to talk about God without using male words. We vitally need some pronouns that will be neutral. I recently counted the male references for God in just the Psalms. Choosing the words "he," "him," and "his". "Lord" and "King", my count was close to 1,311. Maybe we need some of the images we see of God, even if they are inaccurate. Our relationship with God has been created in such a way we can really believe it is God who is directly leading us. It is not magic but it is a mysterious reality.

The Bible says we have been created in "the image of God" (Genesis 1:26-27). I think it is more likely we humans have made God in our image with hands, feet, mouth, voice, gender, and ears. God could not have a body and still be with people all around the world at any given time. God would have to be a spirit, a spirit of love, grace, peace, power, and more. We can sometimes feel the presence of God's spirit in a meeting, at worship, while meditating, or even while watching a rainbow or a sunset. But God is more than a feeling. Sometimes not trying to describe God in detail is a more helpful decision for us. Each of us has an image and concept of what God means to us. I don't think any of us believes God lives in the heavens up there above the blue parchment over this flat earth below. If so, what about the poor Australians down under? Perhaps God is not as personal as we envision God.

Now, I invite you to take a deep breath. I want to introduce a thought about God that could use some conversational interaction.

In ancient times, many people thought some experiences and acts of nature were supernatural. Some would have a sun god, a moon god, or a god of thunder. They had stories to explain lightning, the creation of the world, movement of the sun and stars, and conception of some babies like Hercules, Apollo, and Perseus, who were all fathered by the god Zeus. Even now, there are those who won't start their day until they read their horoscope which is based on the relative movements of the planets. Ancient prophets and even present-day evangelists have declared hurricanes, fatal diseases, and other tragedies were God's way of showing power when humans were grossly sinful. Such doomsayers did not know weather, storms, hurricanes, tornadoes, and even floods are determined by the laws of physics and meteorology which laws, we can believe, were instituted by the Creator God. Even today some insurance companies call natural disasters "acts of God".

Today's twenty-first century humans know about some powers of nature. The people of Joshua's day could believe Joshua's praying, "Sun, stand still at Gibeon, and Moon, in the valley of Aijalon. And **the sun stood still and the moon stopped,**" (Joshua 10:12-13). Today, we know something about the natural forces that keep our solar system moving in an orderly fashion. We would not believe a story of a star leading some people to a house or stopping the movement of sun and moon by a prayer. On rare occasions, two stars or planets may appear to adjoin and glow as one big, bright star. For example, in Minnesota, we could see in the summer of 2015 when Jupiter and Venus overlapped for a few nights. Although Jupiter is 483 million miles away from the earth and Venus is 25.5 million miles away, they appeared as one big star, an amazing sight. My wife Marilyn and I witnessed it from our own front yard.

Many other experiences once considered supernatural are now found to be innate parts of nature. Think of the miracle of a newborn baby. Nine months previously, two hundred million sperm of the father were competing to enter one ovum in the mother's womb or tubes. Now at the moment after birth, the baby, with no coaching or instructions, breathes, coughs, and cries to further expand the lung. If placed on mother's breast, babies instinctively begin suckling and find their first nutritious meal.

Consider for a moment the speed of light always being constantly 186,281 miles per second. Not that we notice, but the light leaving the sun takes eight minutes to reach the earth, ninety-three million miles away. Imagine the complexity of all the stars occupying their gravity-controlled space in the universe. Ships at sea could consistently use the stars to know their location before the advent of GPS from satellites. The accuracy of the table of chemical elements is another amazing natural constant source of information. There are many more elements known today than when I studied chemistry in college in 1948, but the elements have not changed. Just a newer textbook, knowledge has changed.

I am always astounded at the beauty and shapes of the spirals generated by the *chambered nautilus* shellfish. I cannot understand this item of Creation because I am not a mathematician. Almost unchanged in millions of years, each spiraled chamber is created with a predictable formula whereby each successive section of the spiral, if divided into the numerical value of the preceding chamber, the resulting value will always be 1.08. (Remember, I'm not a mathematician). As the chambered nautilus grows larger, it seals off the small chamber and then moves into another larger chamber it had just created as its new home. Another bit of nature having similar or identical unchanging formulas is the sunflower bloom. I hope I can sit at a mathematician's feet some day and really learn the details of the amazing *chambered nautilus.*

Spontaneous healings occur occasionally in medicine. If the patient is a strong Christian believer, they may sincerely believe this healing was an answer to their prayers. Who am I to discourage their belief? Unexpected healings also occur in non-believers. Similarly, other wonderful things happen, such as finding something that was lost, a vision of bright light, or even a bright figure appearing. Amazingly good happenings can often be explained by natural means. Whenever something is found that was lost, such as a hearing-aid or a borrowed book, I thank God for this gift of recovery, although I don't believe God led me to where I had left it. I usually shout out, "Kill the fatted calf! That which was lost has been found!" God and nature gave me a brain which eventually may have led me to my lost article.

I knew a pastor who insisted he always got a parking space downtown Saint Paul by praying for just that. I don't think God is directing traffic, but maybe there is no harm in such a trust. The question may occur to someone asking, "Could it be possible that part of Nature could be part of God? Or could part of God be actually part of Nature?" The gift of eyesight, though often taken for granted, is almost a miraculous and certainly a wonderful gift to us humans. Without any effort on our part, we see before us stereoscopic imaging in full screen and color. The sound is high definition and even synchronized. The scene is automatically focused, dimmed or brightened, and recorded to be seen again and again in our memory. Other senses also are gifts which include sense of hearing, taste, smell, and touch. Our stomachs, bowels, kidneys, livers do their job without our direction. We are thankful for healthcare professionals and need them desperately at times. But many illnesses heal by natural means without the help of medicines or doctors. The beautiful autumn tree colors display without any signal from us. A small acorn grows into a huge, strong oak tree and the shimmering display of moving colors of the *Aurora Borealis* across the northern skies thrills us humans without charge. Sometimes other natural experiences may be interpreted falsely as a miracle, such as I shall now tell you two stories experienced by my family.

When I was about to be born at Mounds Park Hospital in Saint Paul on a cold, December 3rd winter's night, suddenly a dove flew through the open window and landed on my mother's bed. In those days, the heat was controlled by turning the radiator knob in the room left or right or by opening a window that has no screens in the winter. My family all thought it was a sign from God. A dove flying in to my mother's bed! Never were there any special feelings in my own life that would have taken the story very seriously. I think once in a while my parents pampered me in some ways. But on the other hand, I think they really treated all of us four boys with the same love and respect. Maybe it would sound less spiritual if it was a pigeon instead of a dove. The poor bird was just looking for a warm place. The *St. Paul Pioneer Press* published a cartoon of a dove carrying a baby in a baby sheet from its beak saying, "I think I'll go back to carrying olive branches."

The second experience was when I was about fifteen years old, two of my brothers, seventeen and nineteen, and I were in our parents' bedroom downstairs. All of a sudden, we noticed a full moon though the window and it had a white, glowing stream of light going vertically up and down and one going horizontally from side to side exactly in the shape of a cross! It was beautiful! It must be some sort of wondrous sign! We ran outside to see more of it, but outside it was just a full moon. When we returned to the bedroom and looked out, there it was again. So we decided that the glowing cross was the result of the screens' horizontal and vertical gridded reflections making the cross for our eyes to see. It was an exciting moment of joyful exhilaration, but soon the balloon burst and so did our vision.

In the Bible, many dreams are recorded as a message from God, an angel, or a vision considered to be a prophetic mandate for them. Think of Daniel and his dreams and his interpretation of dreams for others. Very few people today interpret dreams as supernatural. Many people have had experiences or visions seeming very real, of a bright light, an out-of-body experience, or a blue light in a tunnel. It might even be an image which is thought to be an angel. I have heard a knock on the door many times, presumably in dreams. No one has been at the door each time. These experiences can come from a lack of oxygen in the brain, certain chemicals, an injury, sometimes the brain and ophthalmic system trying to reproduce a picture of what is happening or it may be just a dream.

Modern people have some understanding of dreams as a natural, corrective brain activity which sometimes can help our brain to ease some conflicts or the result of inner turmoil. Still others represent a desire from within or perhaps have no explanation. Some dreams are wish–fulfillment, others are a spiritual experience. I do not question or doubt their story because they actually experienced it and I cannot deny their experience.

We all have heard some people who have said, "God saved me from a terrible disaster! God made me too late to board Flight 97 to Seattle. That was the very flight that crashed with no survivors!" Such a person may thank God, I know I would, but I could never think that God spared me that flight for my sake. How selfish would that be? I would be grateful for my survival but mourn for those victims' families. Did God ignore them? God doesn't cause airplane accidents or a car crash by a drunk driver. God doesn't send tornadoes over our church or neighborhood or anywhere else. A tornado follows the laws of meteorology. We thank God when the sun shines on our church picnic, but we do not believe that God did that just for us. Sunshine is still a gift from God for which we are thankful. Nature is usually user-friendly by the Creator's sacred intention.

Now, if you are still taking that deep breath, I have another interesting figure about which I have been thinking. (Don't you hate grammar nuts like me who could have said, "which I've been thinking about"?)

We have known her since childhood and now understand her more scientifically. I'm talking about Mother Nature. It is not Jack Frost who colors the trees in autumn. It is Mother Nature draining the chlorophyll from tree leaves and uncovering beautiful yellow, orange, and red images for our eyes and manufacturing photosynthesis to make the oxygen we breathe. All the wonders of nature could be attributed to Mother Nature, but also to God. If we personified all the powers and miracles of nature, I say with tongue-in-cheek, perhaps Mother Nature is actually a Quaternary of our Deity. (It has a nice ring to it). I don't expect the Church to ever change the Trinity belief.

One first step to define the nature of God could be to state *God is Love.* Jesus teaches us to follow the Golden Rule, treating others the way we would like to be treated or sometimes the way _they_ would like to be treated. What are other ways of our describing God? Besides being the Intelligence behind the design of the universe, God could be a Holy Assembly of Concepts and Forces of Righteousness which tend to make the world a better place. We could start with "God is Love," then add "God is Compassion" with a capital "C". The world would be a better place with more love and compassion. Conceivably we could agree that God is... Love. God is Compassion, Forgiveness, Kindness, Grace, Gratitude, Faithfulness. Hope, Generosity, Patience, Joy, Gentleness, Humbleness, Self-control, Friendliness, Warmness, Sense-ofhumor, Self-respect, Cooperativeness, Peacefulness, Creativity, Controlled Ambition, Inspiration, and maybe a trait or two you may add to or subtract from the list. If you have read the above listing rapidly, please read it again slowly. None of the above twenty-three qualities come from science. Nor do they fully define what or who God is. (I forgot to include Honesty.) Science answers some of our questions with knowledge of the marvels of nature, the world, and the universe. no matter how one tries to define God, if we are able to incorporate these attributes of righteousness and transformation into our lives, we will experience great rewards. Our communities, families, and even nations will experience a hint or glimmering of the Nature of God, as well as the Reign of God. We will tend to make the right decisions more frequently. It seems logical we consider making this effort if we Christians want qualities and characteristics pleasing to God or like God. We also pray others will see and reap the benefits for all people.

We can take all these attributes and think of each one as a spirit. By spirits I do not mean ghosts or anything scary. I mean concepts which can become part of a person. Example? The Holy Spirit. Our bodies are temples of the Holy Spirit (I Corinthians 6:19-20), a transformation into righteousness. The Spirit of Love, the Spirit of Compassion, Hope, Forgiveness and think of all the characteristics of a peaceful world and combine them as an integral part of ourselves. The concepts can exist wherever there are people and can be owned by non-religious people as well, making the world a better place. We can expect to be happier with more cooperation, kindness, and peace. In fact, we might find ourselves seeing and experiencing what Jesus described as the Reign of God.

But we cannot pray to a "concept" and concepts don't create universes. Therefore, holding on to our concepts and values, we return to the loving parental image and open our hearts to the One who is as close to what we can imagine is the True God. This brings us back to relating to a loving God, full of grace and mercy. God does exist. God does love us. God works in our lives. We are not able to photograph God. We cannot touch God. Parts of God may not be supernatural. God uses Nature herself to furnish food, livable temperatures, energy, oxygen, and clean water for us humans on earth. God/Nature

11

has given the earth plenty of water, food, clean air, oxygen, and energy directly from the sun. God uses the laws of physics, chemistry, and other sciences to keep us alive and responsible for the future of this earth. The responsibility of keeping the air, waters, and earth compatible with life itself is ours, the duty of us humans. "God's work, our hands."

A nuclear world war could make the earth uninhabitable. Climate-change or overpopulation could also create irretrievable damage to the earth. The power of nature may indeed be a part of our new definition of our God, but God is still greater than any of the definitions we are trying to recognize. If we think about these ideas frequently, in one year we shall have had many opportunities to acquire and use most of these characteristics ourselves, making them parts of our being. We, with God's encouragement, can also change this list for the better at anytime, maybe shorten it a bit.

It's a start.

Chapter Three -
The Nature of Jesus

One of my life-long favorite songs is simply, "Jesus Loves Me".

> "Jesus loves me, this I know, For the Bible tells me so,
> Little ones to him belong. They are weak but he is strong.
> YES, JESUS LOVES ME..."
> (Let's sing it together?)
> (Words: Anna B. Warner, Music: William B. Bradbury.)

My mother's favorite song was a little chorus that went like this:

> "Jesus is the sweetest name I know,
> And he's just the same as his lovely name;
> And that's the reason why I love him so,
> For Jesus is the sweetest name I know."
> (Words and Music: Lela B. Long)

Many years after Mother died, I observed that although I have always loved the song, it seemed a bit shallow to love someone just because they have a sweet name. I'm sure that thought never would have entered my mother's mind. We love, revere, and worship Jesus as Son of God, Master, Savior, Lord, and Christ (the anointed one)! But we are challenged by new information from critical historical and theological studies of the twentieth century. Among them is the discovery of the Dead Sea Scrolls between 1946-1956 and in Nag Hammadi in Egypt in 1945. Also found are several "gospels" with names like the Gospels of Thomas, Peter, Judas, Philip, Mary, and James and also some from detailed manuscripts of antiquity not considered for inclusion in the final canonical Bible. Sometimes we are challenged by our own personal experiences. I don't feel qualified to judge whether Jesus was a human, the Son of God, God since the beginning of Creation, or all three. I believe Jesus, as a human being, had to have forty-six chromosomes in every cell of his body, half from his mother and half from his father. As a doctor, I cannot imagine God or the Holy Spirit having either genitals or a supply of sperm cells or ova, especially in the genealogy of King David. Sperm in semen were first seen through a microscope in the seventeenth century and were thought by some to be parasites and by others to `be homunculi. Each homunculus was a little tiny completely formed baby with all its parts. A woman merely provided the nest where the homunculus would grow into a baby. The writers of the Bible knew nothing about sperm or ova. If Jesus was God living as a human being, how could he possibly feel what it's like to be human? On the cross, he could have just turned off pain for a while. As God, He could have healed all the sick people and not just the several recorded in the Gospels. Trusting the ELCA catch-phrase, "God's Work, Our Hands" could suggest God used Joseph to do God's work of bringing Jesus into this world. God was also present to sanctify the three of them, Mary, Joseph, and Jesus. Would it be difficult for Christians, after all these centuries, to suddenly announce that Jesus was the first-born son of Joseph and Mary with the blessing of the Holy Spirit? We know Jesus was born and raised in a Jewish home. If some of the stories of Christmas are true, it's likely his parents would have treated him differently than his siblings. He was an extraordinary son and was no doubt given a good Jewish education. He studied the Hebrew language as well as the Torah, although he used Aramaic usually in his conversations and sermons. He recalled from memory many quotations from the Hebrew Scriptures. Jesus was a very special man of God, a teacher, preacher, and prophet.

Every Sunday we recite the Apostles' Creed, sometimes automatically without much discernment. My twenty-first century brain finds it hard to believe some of the proclamations. " I believe in Jesus Christ, God's only Son, our Lord." If Jesus is really "God's ONLY Son," then none of us can claim to be God's children, sons and daughters of God, which is a treasured title for us believers. Most likely, in the end, I shall be able to conclude that it works because we are adopted by God in our baptism (or conversion?) as Jesus at his own baptism was adopted when God said, "This is my Son, the Beloved, with whom I am well pleased." (Matt.3:17. also, similarly Luke 3:17).But that still doesn't qualify the rest of us humans to become God's children if we believe, as we say we do in the Creed, "God's only Son".

We profess in the Apostles' Creed, "I believe in Jesus Christ... who was conceived by the Holy Spirit". This is easy to believe if you live in the fourth century. It is also easy to believe if you are certain that God can do <u>anything</u>. Others like me have asked, "Can God really do anything?" Can God sin? Can God place two thousand angels on the head of a pin? Can God make me into a Buick? If God can do anything, why did God permit the Nazis' killing six million Jews in the Holocaust? Could God create, in ten years, another universe like ours which has been evolving for some 13.7 billion years?

Another confession of the Apostles' Creed is "I believe in Jesus Christ... born of the Virgin Mary...". When Isaiah wrote Isaiah 7:14, "Look, the young woman is with child and shall bear a son, and shall name him Immanuel," this is a new translation, the New Revised Standard Version of the Bible. In the old King James Version the Hebrew word, translated from Hebrew to Greek, for "virgin" was mistakenly used. But according to scholars, the Hebrew word definitely meant young woman and not virgin. Matthew, in describing the Christmas story used the Greek word as in the Septuagint, virgin, as a word of prophecy. So that is the word our Creed also says. But Jesus didn't have to be born of a virgin to fulfill prophecy.

Earlier I mentioned my doubts about the Ascension of Jesus story. Gravity would not permit a person to walk on water, but that was not known at the time of Jesus. Not until 1687, when Sir Isaac Newton described the law of gravity would anyone have doubted the ability to rise by supernatural powers up into the heavens. Nor did they know the lack of vital oxygen in the spaces high above the earth. Perhaps Jesus was already in his spiritual body, his soul.

Gravity would not permit a person to walk on water, but that was not known at the time of Jesus.

Another excerpt from the Apostles' Creed is, "The third day he rose again from the dead." Jesus is said to have died on the cross either a little after noon or shortly after 3 P.M. on Friday. He was laid in a tomb by Joseph of Arimathea Friday afternoon and was left alone all day Saturday, as far as we know, because it was the Sabbath. If Jesus was dead from approximately 3 PM on Friday until perhaps 5 AM on Sunday, he would have been dead at least some thirty-eight hours. Now if we all believe God can do anything, there is no conflict. If human bodies are basically the same in this century as in Jesus' time, it would have been impossible to be brought back to life after being dead for so many hours.

One of the most repugnant duties I had as a doctor at Kiomboi Hospital in Tanzania was being requested by the local police to perform an autopsy on a body who apparently had been murdered a few days back. The police wanted to know whether this death was a homicide or some other cause, even natural death. The stench was so bad in our little autopsy room, we opened the door and window, sprinkled some cologne on the floor, and wore two cloth masks. The examinations were done as quickly as possible before starting to feel nauseated. Some of those times I would think about poor Lazarus who "stunketh" because of Jesus' delay in arriving. Truly thankfully, I don't remember a request for this kind autopsy coming more than three or four times a year. Whew! Today with donors of their organs, when they die or even when they are alive, doctors have to know that the timing is very crucial. The organs must be retrieved from the donor, chilled, and sent, by air if not nearby, within several hours to be implanted in the recipient's body or the organs will not survive.

Our Creed declares Jesus was "crucified, dead, and buried". Wasn't Jesus laid in a sepulcher, not buried? Jesus was declared dead by the Roman guards but what if he had been actually in a coma, appearing dead? The Good Friday and Easter stories then become more believable. Jesus arose from his coma in his temporary resting place sometime before Sunday morning and was alive! We can still cry out on Easter Sunday, "Christ is risen! He is risen, indeed!"

The last creedal belief to mention here is "I believe in the… resurrection of the body". I have seen various paintings and cartoons showing bodies rising from graves and passing upward into the sky, as depicted in the Resurrection. We like to think when we die, our soul does go right to heaven. At funerals, frequent mention is made of the deceased "up there looking down at us and smiling." So the loved one is already in heaven in our thoughts at a funeral. It's very comforting. In the resurrection of us all, what about people who were devoured by sharks or certain African tribes' deceased who were left outside to be eaten up by hyenas? And what about cremation that so many people are choosing? Furthermore, those who have lain in graves for centuries are rotted and unrecognizable. Will they all be included in the resurrection? I'm quite sure God has that all figured out. But in the meantime, on Sunday mornings I don't feel inspired by the words, "I believe in the resurrection of the body."

The teachings of Jesus and the example of his life have given us all we need to know for salvation and dedicating our individual selves to God. Through Jesus, we are inspired to love all people and to be kind and more forgiving. We become inspired to be more compassionate in making this world a better place.

"Jesus loves me, this I know, for the Bible tells me so."

Praise God!

Chapter Four -
Atonement

Whenever reading about aboriginal people who thought their gods required a blood sacrifice, I wonder where this idea started. Ancient people were frightened by destructive acts of nature, volcanoes, hail, wind, fatal illnesses, or hurricanes. Many acts of nature were considered punishment from God for humans' sinning. Even today insurance companies sometimes use the phrase "Act of God" for natural disasters.

In the Jewish calendar, every year there is a Day of Atonement. It is called Yom Kippur. On that day, one goat is chosen to make atonement for the peoples' sins. Another goat, the *scapegoat*, was to be let go freely away into the wilderness. (Leviticus 16:6-22). To me, this sounds about as primitive as the ancient pagan practices. A lamb would be sacrificed at Passover. Jesus was crucified at the time of Passover. He came to be known as the *Lamb of God*, the title John the Baptist gave Jesus when they first met at the beginning of Jesus' ministry. (John 1:29).

Our twenty-first century minds have observed the God-of-old as quite different from the God we know today. We believe God does not change, but through the centuries *our understanding of God changes*. In my youth, the God of the Hebrew Bible (the Old Testament) seemed stern, angry, and sometimes unloving. Today, because Jesus has taught us about God's unconditional love, we think of God as a loving parent, full of grace, who loves us always. We don't live in fear of God's bashing us if we make a wrong decision.

"Nothing can separate us from the Love of God in Christ Jesus." (Rom.8:34).

We become reconciled with God when we ask God for forgiveness. We don't need to perform animal sacrifices. It is not so much that Jesus became the sacrifice, once and for all, as most Christians believe. Rather, Jesus was willing to die for us. Through Jesus' example and teachings, we have come to learn of the loving and gracious nature of God. Was not God the same God in the times of Jesus? Did Jesus really have to die to make it possible for God to forgive sins when we turn to God and confess our sins? If the people of Jesus' day had known the loving God of Grace that we now know because of Jesus' teachings and willingness to die for humans' sins, isn't it possible that his suffering and death were really unnecessary?

When Abraham was asked to sacrifice his only son, Isaac, to God, it seemed such a wrong and merciless request. But Abraham was willing to do it and in the end, a divine escape awaited him with an angel's voice and a ram caught in a thicket, available to be a sacrifice. Why was God willing to sacrifice his own Son to fulfill a need for blood sacrifice for all humans to be forgiven? The God we know is full of mercy and would not require a blood sacrifice. People of the first century did not seem to fully know of God's loving grace and unconditional love. God seemed to require the sacrifice of a goat or a lamb before the people could be reconciled with God that isn't the one I know today. God does not want us to sin, but is ready to forgive.

Do you sense a bit of Progressive Revelation in today's understanding of God's grace? I am grateful to Jesus for being willing die for us, but maybe he wouldn't have had to. God is merciful, loving, and has the power to forgive and reconcile us without blood. In the story of the cross, God did not rescue Jesus as Isaac had been released from his challenge by God. On the cross, Jesus, quoting Psalm 22:1, cried "My God, my God, why have you forsaken me?" Jesus did this willingly because as Messiah, he expected to return from heaven within a few years to bring in the Kingdom of God. But that didn't happen. I don't expect the Church or most Christians to totally agree with me and there may be no good reason to change our dogma or creeds. But what harm could come from discussing openly, sincerely, and honestly what Christians are able to believe today?

Some day we shall know the answers to more of these questions. Is this double-talk? Yes and no. What I have just stated as my thoughts can be possibly wrong or possibly right. Maybe in the grand scheme of things, it may not matter that much. We still trust in God. We still believe it is wonderful what Jesus has done for the sake of others and what he has taught us about love, life, faith, hope, generosity, and forgiveness. God's grace is wonderfully and gratefully received by us as a generous gift. We may not now insist that every believer must believe alike in all matters of faith.

In the discussions that may evolve from readers of this book, I would beg to have one rule of courtesy. No one will ever say, "I'm right, you're wrong." There is room for expansion of our ideas of God and eternity. There is room for ambiguity. There is room for some of our doubts.

Atonement is the cancellation of whatever prevents a relationship with God. Atonement is achieving reconciliation with God. It is being "at one with" God. It is a marvelous gift from God! Every day can be *Yom Kippur*, a Day of Atonement.

Chapter Five -
How Does Prayer Work?

What is prayer? Is prayer talking and listening to God? A sacred conversation with one's higher power? The first prayer for many of us might have been every night at bedtime, "Now I lay me down to sleep. I pray Thee, Lord, my soul to keep. If I should die before I wake, I pray Thee Lord, my soul to take. Amen."

When Marilyn and I began having children of our own, we substituted our prayers with something more comforting than "If I should die before I wake…" I would guess that I have prayed at least twice daily most of my life. We can pray anywhere, at any time, in any bodily position and we can believe God is very close to us. Sometimes we may "hear" the still, small voice of God, probably not audibly or literally, but in our mind we have thoughts of what God may be thinking. Before my wife Marilyn's journey into dementia, Marilyn and I started each morning with daily devotions just after breakfast. We usually read from the *Word In Season* from our Lutheran Church and also *The Upper Room* devotional book. We took turns reading and praying and then we prayed together the Lord's Prayer, the modern version. Our before-breakfast table prayer was always, "Lord Jesus, be our Holy Guest, our morning joy, our evening rest. And with our daily bread impart your Love <u>and Peace</u> to every heart. Amen." At the end of this prayer one of us would repeat reflectively, "LOVE and PEACE". We learned this prayer from one of our missionary friends in Tanzania.

One time when our family was living at Iambi, in central Tanzania, I was asked to cover for two Norwegian doctors at Haydom Hospital for a few days while they were going to be gone from their hospital. We were about eight miles from Haydom straight across the African *pori* (wilderness) but about forty miles by the roads, such as they were. The first evening there, I saw a very sick old man who happened to be the local tribal chief. He was suffering from tuberculosis with severe cough, chest pain, and loud noises in his lungs. He was already getting some medicine as ordered. When I returned to my room in the missionary doctor's home, I spent some time on my knees at the foot of my bed, praying something like this.

> "Dear God," I prayed, "Please help us with this *mzee* (old man). Bring your touch of healing for him because he would be such a positive influence on his village if he returned well after having been so sick. If he can be healed, many others will feel secure to come to this hospital with their ailments and hear about Jesus and receive the good care and the Good News that is provided here. Please, Dear God, help us to help him be healed to your ultimate Glory."

I went to sleep and slept peacefully. In the morning, I visited that ward first and asked how Mzee Msaada was doing. The nurse told me, "*Ee, Bwana Daktari, alifariki kama saa nane na nusu usiku.* ("Oh, Doctor, he died about 2:30 during the night.")

I had prayed with all of my heart. I felt so confident that God would heal this important man. I don't think I have ever prayed more earnestly and forcefully than that evening. I thought it was an ideal situation for a miraculous healing. I thought about Jesus saying, "...I tell you, if you ask *anything* of the Father in my name, I will give it to you," (John 14:13-14; 15:7 and Matthew 21:22). It didn't seem to be true for us that night at Haydom.

When our daughter Kathy at age forty-one had cancer which was not amenable to cure, she attended two healing services. One was at a local, popular non-denominational church where a friend who, with good intentions, had invited Kathy to attend a healing service. For me, her father, it was a frightful experience. Standing with us in the aisle, the preacher placed his hands on Kathy's shoulders, started shaking her forcibly, and at the same time in a loud voice began praying. "Father God," he prayed, "Heal Kathy of all her cancer. I command you, cancer demons, to leave Kathy's body right now, in the name of Jesus Christ. Cancer, Leave her body!" All the time shaking her, he then turned to Kathy and quietly asked her if she felt better. When Kathy responded that she didn't feel any different, the pastor began to talk to her about FAITH, as if her faith was weak and therefore not working. I was terribly disappointed in the ineffectively-staged show.

A week later, there was a healing service in the chapel at our own Gustavus Adolphus Lutheran Church. Standing as a family by the altar, in quietness, the pastor anointed Kathy's forehead with oil and said a soft prayer about bringing healing to her and thanking God for always loving and being with Kathy through what she is experiencing. There was a peaceful atmosphere which made it possible for us, her parents, her husband, and siblings to accept that she was in God's hands and God would be with us all through her struggles. She said she felt healed and ready to accept that she will die but she is and will be with God all the time. It was wonderfully consoling.

I absolutely believe in prayer. Prayer is good for us. Prayer adds a new dimension to every thought, concern, or joy in life. But as you might guess, I don't see our prayers, spoken or silent, passing directly "up there" to God. Nor can I understand how God can hear a million prayers from every part of the earth and in every language used by humans. We can always defend God by saying, "But God can do anything." I don't see a lot of prayers being answered as we think they should be answered. So let's talk about it.

Maybe it's a good thing that God doesn't answer every prayer our way. Maybe God knows better than we what we need. "*For your Father knows what you need before you ask...*" (Matt.6:7). Some people are misled when they are told, "Just pray and everything will be all right." It seems to me Jesus was either

25

wrong, miscopied, or misinterpreted when he said, "If you ask me for <u>anything</u>, I will do it."

Truly, if we pray, there is a good chance things will be better. But some things will not be changed by prayer. Prayer is not magic. A hurricane headed towards you a half-mile away is not going to be whisked over to another county just because we prayed. Nor would it always be best if our every prayer was fulfilled.. A cancer that has advanced to stage four and has metastasized to many parts of the body is not apt to go away because we prayed. There are cases of spontaneous cure in severe illnesses like cancer but they aren't necessarily associated with prayers. Prayer is not going to save from financial disaster the one who made very bad investments or gambled much more money than they could afford. But let's not give up on prayer. Prayer does indeed help us. My mother had a plaque on our dining room wall that said, "Prayer Changes Things". Today, I would be more likely to display a plaque that reads, "Prayer Changes Us". Some people, in saying how God works, may suggest "God can do anything." Others might say, in explaining unanswered prayer, "God's time is not our time," or "Maybe God's answer is 'No'." Those kind words may be helpful for some people, but frequently are not helpful comments.

So what really happens when we pray? When I pray silently by myself, my thoughts become calmer and I find I can think more perceptively and with discernment because I prayed. I can think about what I can do to help solve my problem or the concern of someone else. I will become motivated to write a note, make a visit, or send some money. My prayer is directed to God, but God turns it back to me to do what God would want me to do. When Marilyn and I pray for our family, we name them and talk to God about our concerns but we are the ones who are listening to each other. We may then decide to write a letter to our grandson, call our daughter, or send a note of encouragement to my brother. In church, when prayers about various concerns of the Church, a member in need, projects in the neighborhood, nation or world, we get interested in some of those matters. We may volunteer our time or make efforts to encourage or help out. People generally feel encouraged and grateful when they know others are praying for them. The blessings we see would not have happened if we had not prayed.

In the thirteenth century, St. Teresa, a Carmelite nun in Avila, Spain, wrote this somewhat familiar poem:

> "Christ has no body now but yours,
> No hands, no feet on earth but yours,
> Yours are the eyes through which God sees
> Compassion on this world.
> Yours are the feet with which God walks to do good.
> Yours are the hands with which God blesses all the world."

God uses us to do God's will. "God's work, our hands."

When I was a youth in high school and college, I was greatly interested in Billy Graham and his campaigns around the country and world. We even saw him in Moshi, Tanzania. God used hundreds of people to make Billy Graham's crusades so successful. When Billy or George Beverly Shea would say that "prayer was the reason that the campaigns were so successful," they gave God all the credit. I used to wonder how successful they would have been without sending thousands of mailed invitations. They also had arranged well-placed billboards, radio announcements on Christian radio, organized hundreds of groups and individuals to plan and raise money, arranged buses for church groups to attend, and parking for hundreds of cars. Likewise, arrangements were made for the auditorium or stadium to train ushers, educate counselors, organize evangelical pastors to interest their respective members, and arrange mens' and womens' crusade Bible-study meetings. Those seated on stage were instructed to not be looking around, but keep their attention on the speaker or singer on the stage. Billy would wear bright sport jackets and colorful ties and he was a dynamic speaker. Near the end of the service, he prepared the audience for his invitation to receive Jesus as their Savior. Many volunteers waited to serve the people who raised their hands at Billy's invitation and walked down the aisles while the thousands of others were singing softly and prayerfully,

> "Just as I am, without one plea,
> But that Thy blood was shed for me,
> And that Thou bidd'st me come to Thee,
> O Lamb of God, I come! I come." (six verses).

Henry Baker, music; QUEBEC (Hesrerus, words)

Billy Graham was right. God had done all this and should be given the glory. That is how God works, through people doing what seems to be the right thing. "God's work, our hands."

We can still pray to God and tell God what is heavy on our hearts or is joyous beyond measure. We can really believe that we are talking to God when we may actually be addressing our thoughts back to ourselves and our fellow worshippers. So then we decide and discern what we can do with the help of God. If God is not as intimately personal as we have thought, we can return to that personified God and talk and listen and believe. Think of it as praying for a better World and then doing something about it. "PRAYER CHANGES US." We become better people, kinder, more understanding, and more eager to help a needy person because we prayed. Do our prayers go up to heaven? Probably not. But if heaven is where God is, God is right here wherever we are. The Bible says, "God is Love." Could it be said that love is a part of God? God is much more than LOVE but maybe we're getting on the right track.

What if our anthropomorphic idea of God as a Father is right? God would then be a man. He could be only in one place at a time. God is probably neither male nor female. God probably does not have a body. When we speak of God's Hands or God's Voice we are using metaphors to explain the nature of God and God's grace, the way God relates to us humans. We do need God to be someone with whom we can communicate. Therefore, we return to the loving parent image and open our hearts to That One who is as close to what we can imagine is the True God and trust this is the real thing. We are back to relating to a loving God, full of grace and mercy. We are thankful for the love of God and the gift of prayer.

* *

While we are thinking of prayer, please let me share another thought (or SIX thoughts).

SIX Reasons To Like the Modern LORD'S PRAYER

(Traditional version)

Our Father, which art in heaven,
Hallowed be thy name.
Thy Kingdom come; thy will be done on earth as it is in heaven.
Give us this day our daily bread and forgive us our debts (*trespasses*) as we forgive our debtors(*those who trespass against us*).
And lead us not into temptation, but deliver us from evil.
For thine is the kingdom, and the power, and the glory, forever. Amen.

(Modern version)

Our Father in heaven,
Hallowed be your name.
Your Kingdom come; your will be done on earth as in heaven.
Give us today our daily bread.
Forgive us our sins, as we forgive those who sin against us.
Save us from the time of trial, and deliver us from evil.
For the kingdom, the power and the glory are yours, now and forever. Amen.

The Lord's Prayer or the "Our Father" has stood the test of time and is a favorite prayer of most Christians throughout the world in hundreds of languages. In Tanzania, where I have lived, it is called *"Sala ya Bwana" (Prayer of the Lord) or "Baba Yetu"* (Our Father). In my grandparents' Sweden, it is *"Fader Vår"*. Its familiarity rolls off our tongues. We love it. Between church and home, Marilyn and I pray it about ten times every week (We counted). But along comes a new translation which brings it into the language we now speak instead of the ancient English style of speaking. Many Catholics objected to replacing the beautiful Latin of the Mass with English or the vernacular of each country. Some of the older members of my church really did not like it when English was replacing Swedish (God's language) in our worship. But many of our Bibles and hymns have been changed to be more appropriate for modern ears.

Now for those who are on the fence or would like saying the modern Lord's Prayer, here are my six reasons for preferring the new translation:

We no longer use such archaic words as *thou*, art, *thy* and *thine*, so why should we use them in praying? "Our Father in heaven" is easier and clearer to modern ears than "Our Father who (or which) art in heaven".

Today "Forgive us our trespasses" has the connotation of property lines and crossing them more than about sins, errors, or missing the mark. The word "debt" now generally refers to owing money. The word "sin" means to us a transgression of what God has forbidden, "missing the mark," or an omission of what God has commanded. I like "Forgive us our sins, as we forgive those who sin against us." We know what that means.

The reason I prefer "Save us from the time of trial and deliver us from evil" is that when we say, "Lead us not into temptation," it may imply God leads us sometimes into temptation or trial, but does anybody think that God would lead us into temptation? No. The Greek word can mean either trial or temptation. So, I would rather ask God to "Save us from the time of trial". Temptation has a flavor of sexual, dietary, or greedy sins. There are many other trials that could creep into our lives. May God save us from such trials.

"For thine is the kingdom, the power, and the glory." Do you see the incorrect English grammar we've been using for hundreds of years? We're so used to reciting the singular verb "is" it may sound strange to correct it. But one would not say, "These oranges, apples, and bananas is yours." Of course not, because the three fruits are plural. "Yours <u>are</u> the oranges, apples, and bananas" would be correct. Likewise, "For the kingdom, the power, and the glory are yours." Three things are yours. It's interesting that in the old Lutheran Book of Worship (under "Occasional Services"), there occurs a similar mistake. There is a short prayer that is very familiar and which some people pray every day. The problem comes with the part that says, "all honor and glory is yours." Of course, this should be, "All honor and glory are yours" because there are two things, honor and glory, which are plural. But thankfully, after many <u>years</u> of usage, it has finally been corrected in or about the year 2012. Many books still say it the old way. (Aren't you thrilled that you now know this?)

Whenever people from various churches are gathered for worship and pray this prayer, some visitors say "debts" and others "trespasses". There is a cacophony of words that sounds something like "forgive us our tres-debts-passes" as we forgive those-our-who-debtors-trespass against us." The word debt has the connotation of owing money rather than a sin. We can cure that by being willing to choose the new translation.

The last reason is the least important but the new version is slightly shorter by six words and seven seconds of time. (Big Deal.)

So if thou wishest we movest forthward, methinks we are straight-away into Chapter Six, *Sexuality In Church and Personal History.*

Chapter Six -
Sexuality in Church and Personal History

My parents, who had four boys, seemed to believe we should not talk about sex in our house. One day when I was about nine years old, I watched two dogs in our yard doing what dogs do during mating season. As I was leaving the window, I heard my mother ask Daddy if Joey saw the dogs.

My dad replied, "Yes, the damage is already done."

Damage? Damage! It was one good lost opportunity for a short innocuous sex talk. Having three brothers, I knew about male bodies at different stages of development. But I had never seen what a girl looks like "down there" until I started baby-sitting. The first time changing a diaper, it looked funny to me, as if something was missing. I didn't talk to anybody about my discovery. When nocturnal emissions arrived unannounced to me, it was my brothers, not my parents, who told me what wet dreams were and, "Mother knows about it and it's okay if soiled underwear or handkerchiefs are in the laundry."

My mother and I were shopping downtown at the Golden Rule Department Store where she pointed out to me a woman obviously very big in her abdominal area, "See that woman over there? She is going to have baby. That's why her tummy is so big." On another occasion Mother told me a "man gives a seed to his wife and that makes her pregnant and they will have a baby."

Several years later, my brother, Stan, offered to show me how he masturbated. While watching him, I thought he would lose one his seeds and he only had two of them! Also, how can any man, created with only two "seeds" have more than two children? When he ejaculated, I then understood the seed was not a testicle but something in the semen. I still had a lot to learn.

In high school health classes, we learned very little about sex. Somehow, we got mixed messages from school, friends, parents, church, and health text-books. Masturbation is bad. "Touch not the unclean thing" was misinterpreted from the Bible. Rumors instructed masturbation could cause hair to grow on a boy's hands.

Of course, Marilyn and I absolutely knew that we would never have sex before getting married. One evening we were parked in my car by Lake Phalen and I showed her by erection and let her touch it. (She was raised with two sisters and no brothers. But I should have realized, as a nurse, she may have seen and touched many male private parts.) It so happened at that moment a police car with red light flashing stopped directly behind us, the officer walked to the driver's side window and asked me to step out. *Right now?* I thought. After a short delay I stepped out to hear him complain that we were parked on grass and they're trying to keep the grass healthy. But actually and honestly, Marilyn and I were both indeed virgins until our wedding night.

The Christian church developed a negative attitude about sex in the early centuries. They did not inherit it from Judaism, which maintained, "The joy of sex, a joy appropriate even to the holiest days of the week. (Lamm, Rabbi Maurice. "The Jewish Way of Love and Marriage"). The Jewish ritual for males, was based on three duties: providing food, clothing, and a wife's conjugal right to sexual intercourse. (Exodus 21:10-11). In fact, a young man was excused from military duty during the first year of his marriage so he could stay home "to be happy with his wife whom he has taken." (Deuteronomy 24:5). Nevertheless, the early church fathers had very negative ideas. The only acceptable intercourse was one which could lead to a pregnancy and was devoid of pleasure.

In the first few days of the year of my "reading-through-the-Bible-in-one-year," I read in Genesis 4:1, "The man (Adam) knew his wife Eve and she begat their first son, Cain." My first lesson taught me the words "to know" meant Adam had sex with Eve. Later that month in Genesis 38:1-26, I found two convoluted stories involving sex. Judah and his wife Shua had three sons, Er, Onan, and Shelah. Judah's firstborn son, Er married a woman named

Tamar. The Bible says Er was wicked so God killed him, leaving Tamar as a widow. (Verse 8). According to Hebrew laws, when a married man dies without children, his brother must go into the widow for sex in order for the family lineage to go on. So, Judah instructed his son Onan to do just that. Onan obeyed, but when it came time for ejaculation, Onan pulled out and let his semen fall to the ground every time they had sex. This was displeasing to God, so God killed Onan. Later, Tamar, the new widow, was angry with Judah because Judah had not fulfilled his promise to her of marriage to his third son Shela. To get some revenge on Judah, Tamar replaced her mourning clothes with a wrap-around cloth and a veil over her face to look like a prostitute. She waited for Judah to pass by. He stopped and asked her to go with him. Thinking she was a prostitute, he offered a gift of a sheep-kid, but she insisted on a pledge of a signet ring, a cord, and his staff. Months later, Judah heard Tamar had acted as a prostitute somewhere. This angered Judah to the point of requesting to have her killed by fire. Before that happened, she saw him and showed him the signet, the cord, and his staff to let him know the one who fathered her child was the giver of these pledges. Judah became penitent. End of story. (Not quite.)

The son from that sexual contact with Judah was a twin named Perez who is a link in the genealogy of Jesus (Abraham, Isaac, Jacob, Judah. Perez, Hezron...). For many decades of recent centuries, masturbation came to be called "Onanism". Onan's act was not masturbation, but *coitus interruptus*. Nevertheless, masturbation, wrongly called Onanism, "abusing one's self", oral sex, and all non-vaginal intercourse was forbidden. Even in our last century, young boys were told masturbation could cause pimples, hair on the hands, weak eyes, and even such psychiatric illnesses as schizophrenia. Many quoted Bible verses were misinterpreted and used to discourage young boys/men from masturbating. One memorized Bible verse to help stop masturbating was I Corinthians 10:13 NIV (I had memorized the King James version but here is quoted from the New International Version.) "No temptation has overtaken you, except what is common to mankind. And God is faithful; he will not let you be tempted beyond what you can bear. But when you are tempted, he will provide a way out so that you can bear it."

I prayed that verse many times, hoping that would help me stop masturbating. The verse didn't seem to help me. But I must admit I was able to bear it! But in the 1950s, Alfred Kinsey's research in human sexuality discovered most people masturbate without any negative consequences. This knowledge changed the way society, including the Church, taught about sexual subjects.

In medical school, of course, I learned the anatomy and physiology of sex. But after returning from Africa, Marilyn and I attended a four-day eye-opening seminar at the University of Minnesota's Department of Human Sexuality. This course gave us, among other things, insight how important the clitoris was in bringing on orgasms and pleasure to women. That crucial information made me a better doctor and husband. Men with female partners need to be taught the importance of finding and gently stimulating with a finger or tongue that little-understood organ, the clitoris. I was humbled, as a doctor, to have to learn this information so late in my life and career. I was thirty-eight. My wife was able thereafter to enjoy wonderful orgasms until she was eighty-seven years old!

A few months later, in my daily Bible reading, I was shocked to find in the twenty-second book of the Bible, the Song of Solomon, openly describing erotic poetry in most of its eight chapters. There were notes between a man and a woman, two lovers' lyrical words of sexual attraction to each other. Some examples, edited for length, are "How beautiful you are, my love… Your lips are like a crimson thread… Your two breasts are like two fawns… Oh may your breasts be like clusters of the vine… and your kisses like the best wine that goes down smoothly, gliding over lips and teeth." (Song of Solomon Chapter 4:1) The second is similar, "I am my beloved's and his desire is for me. Come, my beloved, let us go out early to the vineyards; there I will give you my love." (Ibid Ch.7-12). My last edited quote is, "Open to me, my love, my dove, my perfect one… I had put off my garment; how could I put it on again?… My beloved thrust his hand into the opening and my inmost being yearned for him. I arose to open to my beloved." (Ibid Chapter 5:2-5).

This is the Bible? I asked myself. But I kept on reading eagerly, finishing the whole book of eight chapters in that one day! When asked, my church leaders told me the Song of Solomon represented Jesus Christ as husband to his bride, the Church. This explanation was never believable to me and therefore I wondered why it is still in our Bibles.

Today there is knowledge about human sexuality, effective birth control, and transmission and treatment of sexually-transmitted diseases (STD). The Church no longer is saying menstruation is a curse or masturbation is "abusing oneself". When I have talked with various pastors and ministers about premarital intercourse, they tell me they don't make an issue of it. While they may not approve, they know most of their church members approaching the pastor for premarital counseling are already sexually and responsibly intimate.

When our oldest son Steve was about twenty-five, he came out to Marilyn and me one Sunday afternoon informing us he was gay. In the late 1970s, neither church nor society had much knowledge about sexual orientation. With hugs and some tears, we assured him of our love. We soon learned very much about LGBTQ (Lesbian, Gay, Bisexual, Transgender, and Queer) at Lutherans Concerned, now called Reconciling Works. (The "Q" was added relatively recently to be an umbrella term for anyone wanting an indefinite term for themselves.) We learned Jesus said nothing about homosexuality. There was no knowledge about sexual orientation until about two centuries ago. No one chooses their sexual orientation or identity. The seven or eight passages of Scripture sometimes called the "Seven Clobber Verses". Though misinterpreted, they are meant to wallop gays and others to believe the Bible "clearly" condemns homosexuality. Now I will list those seven passages with extremely brief explanations inviting you to refer yourselves, if interested, to read them in your Bible at your convenience. By reading those Scripture verses without homophobic misinterpretation, we found the passages are not speaking about sexual orientation as we know it today. They had no way of knowing about loving, caring relationships of many LGBTQ people and the failure of efforts to change sexual orientation in ex-gay ministries or reparative therapy. Then we were able to understand better and early on to celebrate our Steve, his partner, and other LGBTQ people. After living together for twenty-five years, our son Steve and Michael were finally able to get married in Minnesota. This was very good for our family and their marriage enriched all of their lives. Steve and Michael live in their own home near Minnehaha Falls in Minneapolis. We are happy for them.

Well now, Here they are, the seven clobber passages!

1.   Genesis 13:13 and 18:22-19:29. - This is the Sodom story. I hope you can take time to read the whole story from Genesis when you are able. Two male angels, strangers in the city, were invited by Lot to spend the night in his house. However, the men of the city surrounded Lot's house, demanding "to know" the visitors. The Hebrew word, *yatha*, used 933 times in the Old Testament to mean "to get to know" someone is the same word used ten times meaning "to have sex with someone". Scholars have chosen the sexual interpretation not only because of Lot's denial of their request but also Lot's surprising offering of his own two daughters for them to do what the men wanted to do instead of to the two male guests. There was no sex in the Sodom story but attempted gang rape, which would have been evil. The two angel-guests disabled all the men by making them blind. There is a certain falsity in this story. Never in recorded history has there ever been a city in which more than about five percent of its population were gay. Furthermore, most gang rape is performed by heterosexual men as an act of derision and power but not for pleasure or love. Never could it have been "all the men, all the people". The writers of this story had no knowledge of sexual orientation. They knew about male sex in some pagan temples but nothing about sexual orientation. A very similar story in the Book of Judges, Chapter 19 Verses 16-30, about Gibeah and well worthwhile reading to compare with Sodom. The story is about threatened male gang rape, as in Sodom, but here there was a twist. In Gibeah, as a substitute for the male visitors, the host offered to the men his concubine (cohabiting mistress) to do what they wanted to do. The men abused, "ravished," and raped her all night. In the morning, the host found the

woman dead at his doorstep. Most people have probably never heard of the heterosexual sex story of Gibeah.

2. Leviticus 18:22 "You shall not lie with a male as with a female; it is an abomination." - This was one of the many Holiness laws, definitely not approving of male-to-male sex.

3. Other abominations requiring the death sentence include "doing any work on the sabbath" (Exodus 31:15), "any woman charged and proven to be a non-virgin by her bridegroom," and "whoever strikes his father or mother".

4. Romans 1:16-2:1 - The message is not about LGBT people but people, presumed heterosexual, who turned to idolatry, so God gave them up to their lusts, unnatural for them. The passage includes a list of twenty other sins these people committed from murder to judgmentalism.

5. I Corinthians 6:9 - Paul, writing to the Corinthians, is saying the "unrighteous will not inherit the kingdom of God" followed by a list of nine types of sinners. Paul uses two Greek words which, taken together, have been translated with five or six different meanings, one of them meaning homosexuals. Paul wrote in Romans 3:10-23 - "No one is righteous, no not one. For all have sinned and fall short of the glory of God." We are saved by the Grace of God.

6. The "lawless and disobedient" and a list of some fourteen sinners in I Timothy 1:8-10, "...the law is not laid down for the just but including sodomites." Again, we cannot assume such references are relevant for twenty-first century people whose natural sexuality is not in the heterosexual majority.

7. The last passage is Jude 1:7. "Just as Sodom and Gomorrah and the surrounding cities which likewise acted immorally and indulged in unnatural lust, serve as an example by undergoing a punishment of eternal fire." When Jesus talked about Sodom and Gomorrah, he talked only about their sins of inhospitality, not about sexual sins.

Society has good rationale for sensible rules regarding sex to prevent serious problems. Careless, promiscuous, or adulterous sexual activity can lead to disease, unwanted pregnancies, or ruined relationships.

We can thank God for the gift of sexuality. Sex gives us pleasure unlike any other indulgence. From it we receive much joy in having children in our families. We can be thankful that women are beginning to have more equality in issues of sex in homes, the workplace, and in society. We are behooved to treat sex with common sense and responsibility.

Chapter Seven -
What is Salvation?

Throughout my childhood and youth, salvation meant we are saved by the Grace of God through the suffering, death on the cross, and resurrection of Jesus Christ. We are saved from the ultimate result of our sins, punishment in hell. In some churches, salvation happened when a person invited Jesus into their hearts, usually at a tent meeting or evangelistic church service. They would consider themselves "saved" and when you're saved, you know with certainty that you will go to heaven. In other churches, salvation comes at the sacrament of Baptism. It is a gift that the individual didn't earn or deserve, but an act of God's love and grace. That's what we Lutherans believe. Yet we tend to criticize fundamentalist churches that insist a person must do something like "accept Jesus as their Savior," "ask Jesus to come into their hearts," or "believe in the Lord Jesus Christ and you shall be saved" so it seemed to be something they did and not just the Grace of God. We Lutherans are scarcely aware that we provide the sacrament of Baptism (some act we do) to declare the person a child of God. Most people do understand in the baptismal service we are celebrating the Grace of God in transforming this child or adult. We believe if a baby dies shortly after birth and no one has baptized the baby, God's Grace is great enough to save that child. I have baptized many newborn infants who seemed to be failing, but as time passed by, I did it more for the comfort of the parents than the belief it was necessary for the child's eternal salvation.

Lutherans do indeed believe in Grace. Today, baptism of infants is as much for the parents as for the child. The parents are admonished to raise their child in the Christian faith and the youngster will later be asked to repeat the vows made by their parents in their baptism. Today there tends to be a disbelief in Original Sin, meaning that sin came into the world in the Garden of Eden through disobedience of Adam and Eve. When I realized there were people living in Africa, Europe, Asia, even Australia and the Americas thousands of years before Adam and Eve in the fertile crescent of the Middle East, I had to decide the Creation story was not meant to be a historical record. It was rather an explanation of a primitive people trying to explain how they got where they were, how evil came into the world, and something about their relationship to God. There is archeological evidence of murders and therefore sins even in those early appearances of humankind, but sin and evil thoughts and deeds have existed probably always in the human race. So now we believe everyone is capable of sinning and "all have sinned and fall short of the glory of God." (Romans 3:23). It is part of human nature. We all need forgiveness for past sins and sins yet to come. Some people are very proud of their salvation and become judgmental of people who may not have been "saved" in the same way that they have been saved. Unfortunately, neither our baptism nor "being saved" empower us to never sin again. But now we know that nothing can "separate us from the love of God in Christ Jesus our Lord." (Rom.8:38).

Several years ago, I asked my best friend, the late Doug Augustine, a Lutheran pastor and fellow missionary in Tanzania, what he means by "salvation". His answer was, "We are saved to be the best that we can possibly be in how we live our daily life." That didn't sound as spiritual as I expected, yet isn't it true that when we repent and are forgiven of our sins, we are freed to be made whole and able to live the kind of life God would have us live, trusting in God's love, grace, and daily strength? Salvation may not be just an event like baptism or being born again. Salvation may be a process of an entire life of living in the Love and Grace of God, free of guilt, shame, or fear. If there is an afterlife, I have confidence that I will enter into Jesus' presence and be amazed at what I hear and see, especially our daughter Kathy who died at age forty-two. In a Sunday School class for teenagers we were asked what would we like to see in heaven. I remember answering, "a swimming pool filled with ice cream". I am very thankful for a long, interesting, and productive life and I have no fear of death. I know it is possible I will die and then be nothing but a memory in a few people's hearts and minds. I won't know the difference because I'm dead. It would be wonderful to meet my parents, my dear wife, my daughter, and Jesus on that day. I leave that up to God. I know I am a child of God, that I am baptized and therefore "saved". I was saved both ways! Sometimes I feel guilty of selfishness to believe there is an eternal heaven waiting for me. It is much better than a million-dollar lottery surprise! Even if there is no afterlife, I am very grateful for a long, full, and very interesting life with a fine family of four children, six grandchildren, and nine great-grandchildren.

The Hebrew scriptures declare the salvation of God to God's people as a deliverance from the slavery of Egypt, saved from destruction, saved from the Assyrians and Babylonians, and also assurances of future salvation. Now in modern day, there seems to be the assurance that here and now we can live in Christ in this world with blessings of salvation now and the hope of the salvation in the future eternity. But it is not just blessing for the distant future; it is a hope of transformation of our lives right now as we live on earth. God is called "Savior" both by Jews and Christians. We Christians also call Jesus our "Savior" because he was willing to die on the cross and was risen and ascended to heaven and He will return some day in the Second Coming, a time called the Parousia. I personally believe that the "Second Coming" for each of us may be when we die or more likely, Jesus and God are already here on earth helping people to live in love, peace, and harmony. The next subject will be on the Day of Judgment, aka the Second Coming, and Eschatology, the study and belief in the ultimate end of humankind, or about the Kingdom of God on this earth.

Chapter Eight -
The Last Days, Second Coming

Think how many times people have predicted, from Biblical prophecies, dates to expect the Last Days and Christ's second coming to earth and they were wrong every time. I have sort of concluded that it may be more likely "That Day" will never come in the way it is interpreted from the Bible. I believe that the books of Daniel and Revelation have been misleading and misinterpreted by many people from ancient times to the present. Much of the cryptic language of both Daniel and John of Patmos (Revelation) were messages of better days ahead when the Babylonians or the Romans would be defeated. They were writings of hope, a message of warning to repent and be ready for "that day". They were written cryptically so the local people, but not the authorities, would understand what the authors were saying. Even the Qur'an uses the phrase "on that day" some sixty times by my cursory count, seeming to mean "on that day of judgment."

My Aunt Elin belonged to the Wealthy Street Baptist Church in Grand Rapids, Michigan. She used to send us articles and pamphlets about the imminent second Coming of Christ any day now. Every time she visited us in St. Paul, she would tell us about the events of the world at that time which were pointing to Christ's Second Coming. To her, it was very clear. Mussolini in Italy was in the "southern kingdom" and the "Bear of the North" was Russia and Stalin was one beast. She was convinced that Jesus was returning very soon and the antichrist was already living somewhere in India! So there you have it!

We do know, from the science of astronomy, that someday in about five billion years, the sun will have enlarged and be too near the earth for anything living to survive the intense heat. We can hope, if humans do not destroy the essentials of life by nuclear war, overpopulation, or excessive carbon blown into the atmosphere in less than a million years, scientists will find other life-compatible planets and a means of traveling there to save some of the human race.

In today's century, we don't seek meanings out of bizarre dreams. Christians have interpreted Daniel's visions and message to be a prediction that the Temple would be destroyed in 70 A.D. Take the number 70 and say it means 70 years, and 7x70 will be 490 years for the Jewish nation to end their sinning and to be reconciled. 62 x 7 = 434, and three and a half weeks was another number interpreted to mean that Jesus' ministry was three and a half years. See how it all fits together? Yeah, right. I call it manipulation of numbers, like magic. Jesus himself thought and predicted the Messiah would come to earth and begin the kingdom of God by destroying evil and saving the righteous and that would happen in that generation within a few years. But it didn't happen.

Jesus wasn't the only one who predicted wrongly about the Last Days. A pastor-friend of Martin Luther in Lochan thought the end would come on October 19, 1573. Luther himself thought the world could not last more than three hundred more years. He suggested 1540 would be a good year for Christ's return. In the nineteenth century, Baptist preacher William Miller predicted in 1818 that the Second Coming of Christ would be in 1844, calculated from Daniel 8:14.

Edgar Whisenant predicted "88 Reasons Why the Rapture Will Be in 1988". Of course, you've heard of Tim LaHaye's and Larry Jenkins' *Left Behind* series, and Hal Lindsay, who sold twenty-eight million copies of his *The Late Great Planet Earth* with a countdown for Armageddon to be in 1980! It was a best-seller for twenty-one weeks. One would think people would get tired of trying to figure out when and if this is ever going to happen. The reliance on dreams and visions is a pretty tenuous guide and almost unthinkable in the twenty-first century. I say almost because many Christians are still looking for that day. I think there is very little reason to think that someday there will be such a heavenly invasion, destruction of evil people, saving of good people, and then a Kingdom of God on earth.

Barbara Rossing wrote in her book *The Rapture Exposed: The Message of Hope in the Book of Revelation*, "God is coming to heal the world, not to kill millions of people. God loves the world, and God will never leave the world behind." The idea of "Rapture" does not appear in the Bible but the word did spread around the world. The reign of God is among us and God is with us. Our job is to promote the reign of God by doing God's will by caring for the sick, weak, and those in prison, by living in love and grace, and by caring for our neighbor and all people. Immanuel, God with us, in our midst! Revelation promotes both warning and promise. The New Jerusalem, a new world. But "God's work, our hands" will inspire us to be a working part of that new world by doing God's will with our lives.

It might be good for us to listen to Jesus and start assimilating the wonderful qualities we say are God's and God-like and it would be possible for all of us to do this. This, indeed, is more likely to bring God's kingdom here when we all treat each other by the Golden Rule. Jesus said, "The Kingdom of God is within you" or "among you." We pray in the Lord's Prayer, "Thy Kingdom come; thy will be done on earth..." We change our attitudes and maybe some of our beliefs and DO something about it to make it happen. This is not "works-righteousness". It is common sense to value these qualities and both adapt and adopt them for a transformation of human beings' behavior throughout the world. It starts with each of us. We keep in contact with God as we embrace these values and make them part of our lives. God will help us. God will be pleased. We can make a difference. I would love to live in that Kingdom. We pray in the Lord's Prayer, "Thy Kingdom come; thy will be done of earth..."

Daniel, Jesus, Miller, Luther, Whisenant, and Lindsay all got it wrong. Let's see if the kingdom of God can be what we shall have when we walk in Faith, recognizing we do have a calling and responsibility to not get in the way by inflexibility. Think of Barbara Rossing's "Lamb Power". If the reign of God is here and Christ is dwelling with us, we have a paradigm shift in our thinking and now can see the possibilities of human action growing this Kingdom that is already here! We can change for the better. Church can be changed. Our world can be changed. We will recognize it when we experience it. The last words in the book of Revelation are, "Come, Lord Jesus! The grace of the Lord Jesus be with all the saints, Amen."

Chapter Nine -
When All is Said and Done

Sometimes the Church has been slow to accept changes. This is understandable because some changes would interfere with the established dogma and creeds. You may remember how the Church punished Copernicus and Galileo in the sixteenth and seventeenth centuries for daring to describe what they saw in their telescopes about the sun, earth, and universe. Some day there may be a general acceptance of what <u>is</u> true and what <u>may be</u> true and what <u>is not true</u> in theology.

There are still some people who will not accept the overwhelming evidence the Creation of the universe has taken some 13.7 billion years and that humans first appeared here about 70,000 to 100,000 years ago. There are some churches who do not ordain women because Jesus was a man and all twelve of his disciples were men. The fact that the Bible names several women as disciples of Jesus is ignored. Jesus lived in a patriarchal society.

When all is said and done, isn't it wonderful that we who believe in God have more in common than in conflict? Why should any of our differences matter so much in the long run. We love God. God loves us with unconditional love. We want to follow the teachings of Jesus in our lives. We want to treat others kindly and with respect. We agree that love is better than hate. Kindness is better than cruelty. Honesty is more respectable than lying. Generosity is preferable to stinginess. Being satisfied with less is more noble than greed. Forgiveness is more desirable than holding grudges. Peace is finer than war. Cooperation is preferred to stubbornness. Right choices are better than wrong choices. We can make this world a better place.

If you believe Jesus was a human being, I believe Jesus was God, and our neighbor thinks Jesus was both, is there anyone who can prove which is right? What if you believe all the Christmas stories are absolutely, factually true and I believe they are stories, maybe or maybe not literally true but contain a very true message for our understanding the life of Jesus? Could we not discuss and respect each other's opinions?

We can benefit from the inspiring thoughts and feelings we have, thinking of God's Love and our own churches. I feel uplifted after each Sunday morning worship service and empowered by every day morning devotions. I treasure the feeling of love, peace, and the presence of God with me in the sanctuary when our church family is singing, praying, and listening together. You may remember the advice about not taking away a basic tenet of our faith without giving an appropriate belief to replace it. How could we accomplish that? We could collectively state that Jesus was a human being, a Jewish apocalyptic prophet, remarkable and inspired. But there is insufficient reasonable argument or evidence that Jesus was always divine from before Creation, so we replace the dogma with a statement about Jesus' willing sacrifice, tempered with today's understanding of God's sufficient, unconditional grace, mercy, and forgiveness that earlier peoples hadn't yet understood. It could be discussed and perhaps another meaning would be acceptable. This may happen in weeks, decades, or centuries from now. But today, I don't think the Church is ready to be so recklessly progressive as this. I hope I am wrong. Maybe the Church will begin some discussions of faith in the twenty-first century. We would need to understand God in a Christ-like manner. Jesus was willing to obediently sacrifice his life for humankind. Even if the first and fourth centuries' minds had not yet comprehended our present understanding of God's magnificent grace, which would not demand blood sacrifices.

Many of my beliefs are different from my childhood beliefs and are different from many fourth century beliefs, but I feel satisfied that God understands me and my thinking. I think you too can have that satisfaction, support, and strength from what you believe and experience with our mutual Higher Power whom we both call GOD.

In summary, let me tell you how I am keeping faith in this twenty-first century. I thank God, first of all for the messages in the Bible which have influenced my life. I also thank God for the Big Bang explanation, modern knowledge of astronomy such as the movement and balances of stars and planets, and the approximate life-cycle of planets like the earth. I thank God also for natural laws of physics and chemistry such as gravity, verification of death, rainbows, healing processes, the table of elements, the absolute speed of light, and photosynthesis producing oxygen. Science usually is not in conflict with the Bible. If we read the Bible as a collection of stories, teaching us lessons about God and how we can transform our lives, there need not be conflicts between the Bible and our twenty-first century knowledge. I am grateful for God's messages in the Bible. It is good to thank God for every good gift and/or miracle but not to think that our prayers are always answered by God. Good and bad things happen to good and bad people. It is wonderful and peaceful for us to believe we need not fear death and to anticipate entering a wonderful heaven as we leave this life, understanding this possibly may not happen. I want to believe "Faith is the substance of things hoped for," as Paul writes, but it is more than that.

I am keeping faith in God and I believe that Jesus is God's son through his baptism when God said, "This is my son, with whom I am well pleased." I aim to follow Jesus in what he taught us about loving God, ourselves and our neighbor, meaning loving and wishing the very best for everyone we know or meet. I want to model my life by the many concepts of righteousness and what God would like us to become. I believe that God can transform our lives into being much better than we are now. One of our first projects could be trying to design a substitute for war in solving serious international conflicts.

I hope we can have discussions about any questions we may still have, always treating each other with respect. We may disagree at times, but could we all agree in our conversations we shall never say, "I am right. You are wrong." Agree?

LET THE DISCUSSIONS BEGIN!
MAY OUR LOVING GOD BE WITH US ALL.
THANKS BE TO GOD!

We Walk by Faith

We walk by faith and not by sight, no gracious words we hear
of him who spoke as none e'er spoke; yet we believe him near.
We may not touch his hands and side,
nor follow where he trod;
but in his promise, we rejoice,
and cry, "My Lord and God!"
Help then, O Lord, our unbelief
and may our faith abound,
to call on you when you are near and seek where you are found.
And when our life of faith is done in realms of clearer light,
may we behold you as you are, In full and endless sight.
We walk by faith until that day when faith shall be made sight.
-Henry Alford, 1844

About the Author

My name is Joseph Louis Norquist. I go by Joe. I'm a retired family physician and a former medical missionary in Tanzania, East Africa and was born in Saint Paul, Minnesota. My parents were devout, loving second-generation Swedish-American parents. They were members of First Mission Covenant Church in St. Paul. My father, Ernie, was a salesman most of his life. For many years during and after the great depression we were rather poor. He sometimes sang solos in a Baptist church. Mother, Josie, was valedictorian of her high school class but had to work to help support her family so she didn't go to college. She occasionally gave talks to women's church groups. With three boys already, my parents were confident this fourth child would be a girl. They had chosen the name "Joyce Louise" for me. When I was born, I quickly became Joseph Louis. I was the youngest of four boys. All three of my brothers served in the military during the Second World war. Ernest, Jr., who was nine years older than I, volunteered for U.S. Army duty as a medic or chaplain's assistant shortly before Pearl Harbor. As a pacifist, he did not want to be drafted and have to carry a weapon. He became a prisoner-of-war of the Japanese in WWII for three and a half years in the Philippines, struggled through the infamous Bataan Death March, and then was shipped to Japan. After the war, he studied theology at Princeton Seminary in Princeton, N.J. and Lund University in Sweden to become a Presbyterian minister for many years. He was much involved with the civil rights movement. Then Paul, four years older than I, served in WWII on an aircraft carrier, became an aeronautical engineer for Lockheed in Burbank, CA. Third was Stanley, two years older than I, who served in the U.S Cavalry in WWII and after that went through medical school. He moved to Longview, Washington as a family doctor. I am the only surviving brother.

With a strict but kind conservative upbringing, we didn't go to movies nor did we dance. There was no alcohol in our home, no gambling, and no heavy work on Sunday. We didn't even say "gee," "golly," "heck," or "darn". I fully believed the Bible to be inerrant, meaning the Bible could contain no errors or mistakes.

When I was twelve years old, during a Sunday evening service at Como Park Covenant Church in St. Paul, kneeling by a front pew, I offered my life to Jesus for wherever God could use me. In the teachings of my church, this act could be called "getting saved" or being "born again". Volunteering for Youth for Christ and Billy Graham campaigns in the Twin Cities seemed to bring me closer to God. Having heard three missionaries speak at my church about their work in Alaska, China, and Belgian Congo, respectively, I felt a calling from God to be a missionary. In high school it felt like a real, divine message to me from God. After high school, I entered a pre-seminary course at the University of Minnesota. My mother had died of a heart attack at age fifty-one, when I was sixteen. Father died two years later of a stroke at age fifty-two, when I was eighteen.

After two years in college, I had to choose an academic major for the next biennium. What's a good major for mission work? Could it be anthropology? history? archeology? philosophy? I had already studied English, speech, history, radio speech, and two years of Classical Greek where we read The Odyssey instead of the New Testament. We did read the Gospel of John in Greek. My med-student brother Stanley asked if I had ever thought about going as a doctor. I hadn't, but considered the idea appropriate for mission work. I enrolled in two pre-med courses, inorganic chemistry and zoology and loved them both. So, I chose pre-med as my major, continuing on through medical school. I've never been sorry for that decision.

In June, 1953, I graduated from the University of Minnesota Medical School. One week later, my wonderful fiancée Marilyn Larson and I were married and I became a Lutheran. Three days later, Marilyn and I were off to

Washington, D.C. for my one-year internship at Walter Reed Hospital. Since Marilyn was an R.N., she worked at Walter Reed. Our first-born son Steve was born at Walter Reed in 1954. Steve's life has been filled with music, piano, choir, and musicology. Our next U.S. Army assignment for two years was Eielson Air Force Base near Fairbanks, Alaska. Alaska was still a territory in 1954 and was considered overseas duty. Our second child Kathy was born in 1956 during our Alaskan assignment. She was a wonderful daughter with a beautiful soprano solo voice. Unfortunately, she died of cancer at age forty-two.

The curious darkness of the midnight sun and the breath-taking beauty of the shimmering Northern Lights overhead were especially meaningful to us. Living in "the last frontier" and experiencing -52°F temperatures were uniquely stimulating for us. Did I say stimulating? It was bone-chilling cold. The opportunity of being commanding officer of a medical detachment to the 4th battalion enabled me with leadership skills for becoming doctor-in-charge of two hospitals later in Africa. I moved to Thief River Falls in northwest Minnesota for two years to gain surgical experience for Africa. The clinic I was joining had one surgeon and three family doctors who preferred not to assist in surgery, giving me the opportunity of assisting in many operations.

We joined the First Lutheran Church in Thief River Falls, belonging to the Augustana Synod. Our commission to serve as medical missionaries in Tanganyika, East Africa took place in St. Paul in 1958. We then crossed the Atlantic on the old *Queen Mary* in third class. It was a large cruise ship, think "Titanic". A six-month required course in tropical diseases at the University of London School of Tropical Medicine was completed. We left for Tanganyika on a one-class British ship, the *Kenya Castle*. Sailing west from Genoa, Italy, we crossed to where the Mediterranean Sea meets the Suez Canal. Continuing through the Suez Canal and Red Sea to the Indian Ocean, we finally reached our destination, Dar es Salaam, Tanganyika on the east shoreline of Africa, some four hundred miles south of the Equator. Shortly after that initial voyage, missionaries switched to air travel rather than by sea, arriving in hours rather than weeks at our destinations.

Our home for the next six-and-a-half years was at Iambi and Kiomboi Hospitals in the Central Region of Tanganyika. Tanganyika became independent from Great Britain in 1961 and united with the island of Zanzibar the following year. By combining letters from each country's name, the newly-formed nation became TANZANIA, borrowing "TAN" from Tanganyika and "ZAN" from Zanzibar. The variety of experiences, both medical and cultural, led us to many friendships and opportunities to treat unusual sicknesses. I was expected to do some surgery for which I was not specifically prepared. With some helpful teaching from ophthalmologist, Dr. Frank Adair from St. Paul, I learned some easy steps in doing at least one hundred and fifty cataract operations.

Our third child, Judy, was born at Kiomboi in 1960. Judy became a legal secretary but decided that wasn't for her. To our thankful delight, she and her husband Mike have lived close-by in Minneapolis for much of their married life. Our fourth child, Doug, was born during furlough in Minnesota, in 1962, six weeks before we all returned for our second term. Doug became a Lutheran pastor and now lives in the Upper Peninsula of Michigan. Marilyn and I are both convinced those seven years of medical missions work in Tanzania were by far the best years of our lives. Some of my faith-journey stories in Africa are in this book.

After Tanzania, our next twenty-eight years were lived in St. Paul, Minnesota, where I worked as a family doctor in St. Paul's East Side and Maplewood, a large suburb of St. Paul. In those earlier days, family doctors made house calls, delivered babies, and assisted in surgery with their patients.

We loved to travel to places like Norway, Sweden, Hawai'i, Australia, and around the U.S.A. My main hobby was model rail-roading. My avocation for some twenty-five years was producing some fourteen 16-mm movies and videos for non-profit organizations. Among them were Global Health Ministries, Lutherans Concerned, the Minnesota Orchestra, Merrick Community Center, St. John's Hospital, and several churches.

Since 1965, we have been very active in our Gustavus Adolphus Lutheran Church, Marilyn's childhood church in St. Paul. I was not a teacher, but I did volunteer as a mentor to first-year medical students for some ten years. I was on the Minnesota State Board for Community Colleges for seven years and Merrick Community Services Board for four years. Most of my life experiences have broadened my education.

My motivation for writing this book came from my interest in learning more about God. I used to enjoy going through the stacks at the university's library and be thrilled by the immense knowledge stored in such a place. In this book, I am avoiding deep theological studies and describing more personally how I have dealt with the questions and doubts as they came to me.

I hope this book will encourage conversations in our churches as we bring the fourth century up to the twenty-first century. I am not going to try to change peoples' minds necessarily, but I do think it is time we at least discuss questions with mutual respect and avoiding anyone's ever saying, "I'm right. You're wrong". Thank you for reading this author's page. Dr. Joe